My First Bible

The Baby in t

Kathy Lee and Roma Bishop

Little EAGLE

Miriam was very excited.
She had a new baby brother!
But her father didn't look happy.
Her mother was frightened.
'Miriam,' they whispered,
'don't tell anyone about our baby.'

'The king of Egypt hates our people,'
said Miriam's mother.
'He has told his soldiers
to take all the Hebrew baby boys
and throw them into the river!'

So Miriam's family kept their baby hidden.
They never took him outside.
No one knew about him.

But as the baby grew bigger,
his voice got louder.
Miriam felt scared.
Someone might hear him crying…

Then Miriam's mother had an idea.
She made a little basket shaped like a boat.
She covered it with waterproof tar.
It was just big enough to hold a baby.

The baby's mother gently put him in the basket and carried him down to the river.
She hid him in the reeds by the water's edge.

Suddenly Miriam heard people talking.
She peeped out from her hiding place
and saw a lady wearing gold and jewels.

It was an Egyptian princess,
the king's daughter.
As she came down to the river,
she noticed the little basket.
She wondered what it could be.

Then Miriam ran to fetch her own mother.
Now she could look after her baby safely.
God had kept Miriam's brother safe.

The baby lived with his own family
until he was old enough
to live at the palace with the princess.

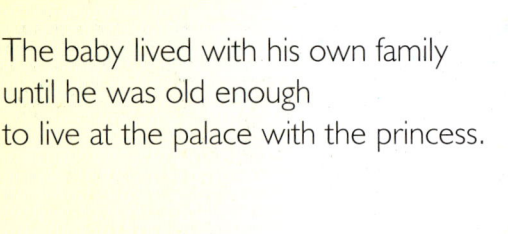

His name was Moses.
When he became a man,
he helped his people to escape
from the king of Egypt.
And God always looked after Moses.

This story can be found
in the Bible in Exodus 2:1-10

Published in the UK by Eagle Publishing
PO Box 530, Guildford, Surrey GU2 4FH
ISBN 0 86347 433 0

First edition 2001

Copyright © 2001 AD Publishing Services Ltd
1 Churchgates, The Wilderness, Berkhamsted, Herts HP4 2UB
Text copyright © 2001 Kathy Lee
Illustrations copyright © 2001 Roma Bishop

All rights reserved

Printed and bound in Malta